A Devil Every Day

A Devil Every Day

John Nyman

Palimpsest Press
1171 Eastlawn Ave.
Windsor, Ontario. N8S 3J1
www.palimpsestpress.ca

Printed and bound in Canada
Cover design and book typography by Ellie Hastings
Edited by Jim Johnstone

Palimpsest Press would like to thank the Canada Council for the Arts and
the Ontario Arts Council for their support of our publishing program. We
also acknowledge the assistance of the Government of Ontario through
the Ontario Book Publishing Tax Credit.

Canada

LIBRARY AND ARCHIVES CANADA CATALOGUING IN PUBLICATION DEDICATION

TITLE: A devil every day / John Nyman.
NAMES: Nyman, John, author.
DESCRIPTION: Poems.
IDENTIfiERS: Canadiana (print) 20230150837
            Canadiana (ebook) 20230150853

ISBN 9781990293467 (SOFTCOVER)
ISBN 9781990293474 (EPUB)
CLASSIfiCATION: LCC PS8627.Y52 D48 2023 | DDC C811/.6—DC23

for Dad—thanks for tending the plants

```
 _,    \|/  i
  =^ v ^  / ==
 =cx+ = x< <  ‾  ‾
–,\ __| |E / /  .y__
<===-VV  /v=\ \––’
 <=‘e ^@<====>
 <=/ / / /V^\ \
  / /l. /    \\\<




                          c(  \
                        r C )ci o_
                        ( < )*Q<`
                        v/__rO. )
                             (__)




               .         ^
              A ,   n | \    .
               \ r\ |  \ / / / /
                \ \ \i ) f )/ /
            . ~ --- ,__\ ,)(  / /
        .  ~ - - - .  --*O>- ,___
          >-~H ^v / |\\ \- . ._  ~,
           < ~/ // | |v  \_)     `
            u^V|  /  )U
                    V U
```

```
           ||,
         - U *}
  .    < ~  } r r~, //_ e
_>\{  , _<  | || I ~ ~ _<
~=`  :`  J- ~  Vv \\ \\
}~C k ~ | ,.AE~r
    ~= >  <,  ` <,
   _*~  o ~`  , ,\
   `  ~~  }< }`
    `  ~ ~  {~,}




                \
                \\    ^     ,  h   /
                 \\   \\  //  )\\  ||
          n_  \\  \\  (( X \\  ||
~------_>-\\  )? |X_ >\\ |\
           `  ~>@KK=__=>W====~~ , --
            _~ `  /A\ n ,~=    =__
         ~`      //  \\ \\ \\        = _
       //       //   \\ \\ ),         =>
              ||    ((,\\
```

Contents

But if all are alike both right and wrong, one who believes this can neither speak nor say anything intelligible; for he says at the same time both 'yes' and 'no.' And if he makes no judgement but thinks and does not think, indifferently, what difference will there be between him and the plants?

—Aristotle, *Metaphysics*

If you were to listen to his arguments, at first they'd strike you as totally ridiculous [...]. But if you see them when they open up [...], if you go behind their surface, you'll realize that no other arguments make any sense.

—Plato, *Symposium*

Becoming

The Devil Writing

The Devil is not exactly
an author

He doesn't write a word
unless you're speaking

And he doesn't mind repeating

But he also doesn't hesitate
to falsify

He knows that talk is cheap,
though speech is free

He's fluent, but obtusely

Perhaps his evil's mostly
just banality

The Devil writes poetry
at the poetry reading

His ethics is doing it my way

I
to a houseplant

Whoever wrote *Beyond Good and Evil*
must have had a tree stuck in his brain,

the way your brethren rise up topsy-turvy
to shunt themselves away from gravity.

My species keeps its evil in statistics,
our reptile selves careening aggregate

towards the Devil, while yours accepts it's mindless
at the level of the individual.

Unless your kingdom's individual
thinks at scales too miniature for me,

or vegetable ethics tend to draw a line
too fine to be engraved on lumber's textiles,

too unlike the I that shoots like a poplar
from the baseline of my word processor.

When I Roll Downhill

My thought makes worlds, my finger subjects,
but they rarely point in the same direction

these days, when joining mouth and money
makes you an auctioneer. All evil

comes with, on the front end, good.
Meanwhile, goodness is cavalier

in the Janus-face of its own denial,
and the Devil wags his index forever

elsewhere. Maybe I'm cynical—who knows?
Maybe I'm saying both 'yes' and 'no.'

Maybe I've planted myself in this circumstance.
Maybe I'm rooted. Maybe I'm colonial.

A man likes to stand on the slope of history
that tilts to the future. He likes that control

over time, and could always use a little more.
But wrinkling my brow to look forward just fucks up

my footing, and when I roll downhill I'm looking
backwards as much as at what I'm headed for.

Backwards Aphorisms

A man is a backwards-walking animal.

> *It feels like I only go backwards.*
> *Every part of me says, "Go ahead."*

2) Judge an action by its outcome, not its intention.
1) A judgement is an action.

> When Earth blurs lines, Heaven sharpens them.

He pulled the mirrors off his Cadillac,
'cause he doesn't like it looking like he looks back.

> Unlike intelligence, wisdom works just as well
> backwards as forwards.

Collaboration

to a houseplant

My vegetable thoughts glow a mineral colour,
common and cobblestone. They come
from a country cached deeper than the middle
of me, yet also skin-deep—as deep
as the ocean between.

My vegetable thoughts keep me waiting for you
to unspeak all my symbols, my IDs,
to be "you" merely, the yet-to-be
of a waypoint leading to "me."

My vegetable thoughts call the constellations
by Latinate names, though the light is the same
in stories you've inspired my fathers to erase,
your blank striving guiding the colonizing shape
I trace through my maleficent bloodline.

My vegetable thoughts hope you'll help me justify
parroting mistranslations of starlight
whose origins, by the time I arrive,
will have long since been destroyed.

Life-Death

When Dad insists he might revive
this litter,

and I've arrived at taking out
its light

—my aloe's broken fellow slowly
losing

its hold on its own inanimate form
of alive

(later, I'll find out Dad's got it
replanted

and, of course, I'm wrong; the remnant
thrives)—

I think of that bare stranger from
the movie

who engraved a mystic symbol into
flesh

—XXXII (age of
the risen)—

and split another aloe's flattened
lifeline

to cool the burn scars sprouting
on his back;

there was still an entire lifetime to go
for him.

When the burning plays again on
the projector,

and I wince and wonder, and suffer, but also
forget

that aloe, I know there's always more
than life-death;

there's at least this taxing affect, its damage
and debt.

White Mood

Sometimes I show up white as sunlight,
brittle as eggshell and sticky as bird shit,

my mind brandished and a long word cocked
in the infinite conflict of keeping it open.

Sometimes my white mood shines knifelike
and steals freely, blotting another broad leaf.

Sometimes it flies like a white flag, entreating
no contest—in other words, putting a stop to this.

Ossified, spinal, my white mood slips straight through
my doubleness, urging my brain and my body

to unify, even while assuming they're separate.
Sometimes I think it's a little like whiteness

mimics the late-season sunbeams, splitting
the fruit from the flower, my white mood aggrandizing

life with a label life's not—and maybe
I'm proud of it. But sometimes my white mood loses

the wager it's made on my ancestry, squeezing me
gummy as school glue, the ghost of atrocious

biologies. Sometimes my white mood's ridiculous,
I admit, and I have no excuses left for it.

The Devil's Mind

The Devil isn't comfortable
with ignorance

But that's not the same as trying
to really see

The Devil only speaks thanks to
his thoughtlessness

He'd always rather chat
than get to working

And though his talk is cheap,
it isn't free

Even the Devil needs money

The Devil's not unconscious
of his ignorance

But that's not the same as wanting
to know more

Still, it's not the Devil's fault
he's silent

Or complicit in hierarchies
he won't enforce

He only tallies scores

The Devil's mind is closed
to ignorance

But that's not the same as opening
one's eyes

In fact, the Devil sees himself
as blind

And just, and justified

And yes, it's true: the Devil's
white

But he doesn't care that he is—
do you?

Myself, I care about what I do

Seed Ball

Most of my dreams and detours are with you,
packed in there with everyone else's.

Most of the remainder are strewn across continents,
unless they've grown up into the spindly

branches whose skinny assertions stand
for what I've already accomplished.

I'm surprised to find myself the oldest
thing alive or that died in my bedroom,

but your surprises are thick and rippling
with true astonishment, a bullish expectancy

here already. Never mind the risk
of slow explosions, or collapsing beneath

the overflowing number of dispersion—

I believe seeds are the peak of life,
higher than any old propulsion.

Mine, I'll sing like a troll in daylight,
clamour them fat as the ocean.

Sunlight
to a houseplant

You'd think I'd give acres
for a part whose government
demands ascension to the seat
that's nearest the sun's,

as if the scalar measure by itself
farmed up the carrot, clasped the stick,
and drove the steel-hot carriage.

In truth I fill a radiating flesh,
strain the many tendons
of my hand to blindside brightness
and decide, then cobble a different labour.

Meanwhile, basking, you command a demigod's
annoyance from the celebrated fortress
that shines right in my eye.

Telescope the sight that turns a circling
perspective to a meteorite: no longer
are the blind found in darkness,
but in yellow noontime's night.

Celebrate

Celebrate stillness,
okay?

Celebrate staying
the same. Celebrate

holding your body's own
embodiment

—as it is, and not
utopian.

Be sure to celebrate
the opposite. Take care

to take no ownership,
celebrate impulses

less unwilled
than will-less.

Celebrate contradicting
the topic.

Shut up and
celebrate. Celebrate

long and often.

I

to a houseplant

For all the slowness of my knowing,
you must be laughing as you daughter
and I'm stuck thinking of *I* as a father.

Not like the link in a bloodline, no—
like the source of a soul, like its soleness,
its wholeness, or maybe its hole:

ego, anxious for doles of emotion
from Facebook, lacking its swarming libido.
Even hedonism might have to work harder

to break itself free of the extremist box
and win its logic back from the cropper.
But you, with an extra extremity, already matter

twice, like irony finally defined.
You split up your selfhood like fodder. You
are alive, but without being like.

ID: becoming plant

I might write the "dynamic, turbulent form
between perfect chaos and perfect order,"[1]

where "all directions of motion and rhythm
will be equally probable,"[2] but not without
my own idiosyncrasy.

My poetry might "articulate itself through a body
that sees itself as irreducibly relational

to material forces,"[3] but it's unlikely
without an idea, an eye from which
I see.

My ideas might "enter into composition with *something else*
in such a way that the particles emitted
from the aggregate thus composed will *verb vegetally*,"[4]
if my id is disciplined to isolate a vegetality
that's "unique."[5]

But I might still be an idiot, knowing, but not yet doing
what your bodies can do.[6] And so,

1 Catanzano, Amy. "'Fractal Poetics': A Rose is a Leaf is a Rose is a Leaf." *Jacket2*.
2 Fulton, Alice. "Of Formal, Free, and Fractal Verse: Singing the Body Eclectic."
Conversant Essays: Contemporary Poets on Poetry.
3 L'Abbé, Sonnet. "A Botany of My Breath in Five Flowerings." *Open Letter* 13.9.
4 Houle, Karen. "Animal, Vegetable, Mineral: Ethics as Extension or Becoming?
The Case of Becoming-Plant." *Journal for Critical Animal Studies* IX.1.
5 Ibid.
6 Cf. Gilles Deleuze, *Spinoza*: "we do not even know what a body can do."

I'll philosophize in my own idiom[7]
second, if first
I split my idiom with you.

---

7 See Catherine Malabou, *The Future of Hegel.*

Becoming Evil

New Binaries

Someone said "the other side" and I pressed it
into my palm and ushered them out.

I was fearful I'd be outmoded, known
as a binarist when I wasn't—it's simple

as yes or no. I realize you don't
flip coins the way I do, but I've caught you

defending your circle's faces regardless.
I've never been that close to anyone.

Then again, I take "close" to be relative
and haven't been liquid for ten thousand sunsets;

I've been swimming and gorging myself on the dark.
I am so tired of talking across

the pie chart to you. I want to blow up
into one. I want to fall apart.

The Devil's People

By law, the Devil is no one
unusual

Our government calls him
an individual

He pays the same money
the rest of us pay

As long as we're free and equal

The Devil's no more than a man
of the people

No more than a bearer of rights
unimpeachable

The difference is, the Devil knows
true freedom—

The freedom to be evil

Laughable Aphorisms

Poets play the shepherds of the world, but really they're the fleece.

Saying is saying—not doing, not being. Saying is saying is saying.

Say "irony," though, and become ironic.

I know what it's like, not what it is.

But why create something when there could be nothing?

The Devil

The Devil doesn't care about reality,
just dreams

He's sleeping through your confrontations
with authority

The Devil seems
innocent

He isn't
investigated

The Devil knows that evil's
unintended—

You don't have to tell me

The Devil's Song

The Devil says his business
is his song

The Devil makes it up
as he goes along

He's evil, but he isn't
wrong

He just goes on too long

The Devil shits on life—he likes
survival best

But he's not made of stone—
he has engagements

The Devil isn't fake—
he's naked

Otherwise I'm only clothes

The Devil's Fire

The Devil's tell is smoking
on the regular

He loves a habit—he'll probably burn
forever

He still puts petrol
on his lips

And when he speaks he spits

Remember: the Devil
is reptilian

Of course he shits on life—he lives
in Hell

He's money-poor, but rich
in scalps

My head is somewhere else

New Normal

Eyes are now stronger than bone,
but they still see us black and white.
The sun has been trumped by a wall
and the blind and backwards world.

A lot of the hallmarks of progress
have clawed themselves back in a tangle.
They offer up thumbs like a succulent
to soothe each burning injustice.

But their wet and spiny universe,
under observation, is spineless.
In the meantime, counting the ashes,
I fell smaller into myself.

I Am

Smaller than a pinhead
Smaller than life's chemical
        constituents
Smaller than a trace amount
Smaller than the shadow
        of a doubt
Smaller than a rumour
        on the wind, and
        the wind itself
Smaller than the calculus
        that draws the truth out
Smaller than its digits
Smaller, of course, than zero
Smaller than the difference
        between power
        and symbol
Smaller than my implications
Smaller than the singular
Smaller than you and I,
        too, and
Smaller than you

I Am

I am the master of my actions.
I hold on to a pound of privilege
tight as a tug-of-war.

But I'm in no mood for winning,
I just try to hold the score.

A corpus of inconceivable people,
the way I know myself in every
sense but actual substance—

at least I have something to take care of.
I am less, but not heartless.

The Likeable Devil

Is it wrong to find a virtue
in the Devil?

He only addresses one thing
at a time

Hypocrisy emerges
in the long run

But hypocrisy isn't a lie

Is it wrong to find two faces
more attractive?

A double-cross has bright spots
of its own

When one of the Devil's faces
speaks to you

I'm speaking to you alone

The Friendly Devil

The Devil doesn't want
what you ought not to

But he doesn't always want
what he gets

The Devil lives to serve
the contract

And does just what it says

The Devil gives you space—he takes
you home

And leaves his baggage on
your doorstep

He never holds
his own

But at least the Devil has somewhere
to go

He isn't made of stone

Touch-Me-Not

Somebody coded the system for tragedy.
Now it wants sadnesses played on a loop—
a snuff film for the rest of our lives.
What happened to good old entertainment?
Where a red shirt got shot down for no good reason,
and a lover was a trophy or an insult, and our daddies'
balls dangled, and they sluffed the hypocrisy?

These days, humanity folds in my wallet
for point-of-sale virtue signalling. My buddy
makes faces, moans "Oh no!," and mimes reprimand
when I slap at my sensitive plant. But trust me:
its shrinking is just a dumb atrophy, same
if it's living or dead. And this, this
is comedy! Watch, and I'll do it again.

The Devil's Intelligence

The Devil loves a panoply
of wrongthink

But he doesn't think too much
himself

He breathes hot air, and then
he breathes it out

His thoughts are made in his mouth

The Devil's intelligence comes
with no capacity

Where speech is free, he picks up talk
for cheap

But the Devil hasn't practiced
what he's preached

Instead, he just repeats

Since no one trusts his word, he trusts
in writing

In writing, his meaning comes across
absurd

Unless he means exactly
what you've heard

It's Mine

Nonsense is getting familiar.
Its currents are throwing
overstated flames
straight at a concrete face.

It's my face, stopped mid-yawn
like Ducreux's in a memeless experiment,
trollishly blowing my cheek up
full of an ear fold.

I'm stuck in your terracotta army.
I'm listening, but long-since informed and indifferent.
My fire's a secret, and I'm sticking it
out alone.

You're tanked on talking big
and taking care of yourself;
go home. It's I
who defines life. It's mine.

The Devil In Person

The Devil's clothed in nothing-
coloured skin

The Devil's naked—he isn't
faking it

It's just a character
he's in—

A sinister person, with a person's
rights

His pattern's not abusive
every time

Although he doesn't empathize,
he finds

That I'm completely justified

Horns

I've heard a story, from the victors' side,
        about a few deluded anti-Semites

Who'd say that Jews had horns, then say no more,
        except to apologize after they'd been dunked on.

I must be blessed by God to never have to
        question the kind of imbecility

A person ½ like me can counter-argue
        by pointing at their scalp unthinkingly.

The thing is, no one has ever tried me,
        so I never actually thought the delusion was normal,

Though the saying goes that I chose
        to say nothing when they came for someone else,

Then someone more, so that when they came
        for me, I had no one. Unless—was it me

        who had always been coming?
It might be a question of whether or not I'm normal,

Of ½ a lifetime pulling out my hair
        to cordon off its cowlick waterspout

And tame the waves I trace for Devil horns.
        Where I come from, a ½ Jew is an insult

To centring the marginalized—
  which isn't meant to blame those who identify,

It's just an act of silencing.
  Lucky one prong's only ½ about me

And the other's just a matter of gravity:
  "How does your hair stick up like that?"

  "Oh, it does that normally."

Me

Same old frozen explosion,
forever these two extremes,
mouth-deep in a mock combat,
hedonic on repeat.

Revolution slow as holy
water exiting a cup,
chemistry's miraculous showboat,
reconfiguration of matter.

Lovely how the quickest virtues
ground themselves in the middle way.
Judgement's free, but change is shackled
to me, depressed between the bed sheets.

Praise God

Trinities

God commands "no"
Gaia says yes
The Devil is in between

God is the dreamer
Gaia, the bed
The Devil is the dream

God is violence
Gaia's sex
The Devil? He's obscene

God is the Other
Gaia, one
The Devil must be me

Sad Aphorisms

First ethics: be a weak enemy.

There are two world views: either you think you're not good enough for this earth, or you think you're too good.

Please, keep your thoughts as small as you are.

The best you can be for others is their background.

You hear what you want to hear, and you hear what you don't want to hear.

Nobody wants us except each other.

The Devil's Soul

The Devil only breathes smoke,
never fire

His sentiment smoulders, but the flame
isn't there

That's why he'd rather be rigorous
than right

What matters to him is air

The Devil doesn't demand that you suffer,
he only ever asks

He reassures you with his words,
condemns you with his acts

It's like he leaves a like
but takes it back

The double-take a trap

The Devil's a Cheshire cat smile,
but serpentine

He passes time building a maze
in place of his soul

While yours he'll treasure
even when no one else does

I'm unsure about my own

Wikihole
hundreds of open windows

A Whitman initiate, I contain multitudes.
Picture the hundreds of tabs in my browser
suspended from history, half-scrolled, in need
of reloading: my soul as recalcitrant wikihole,

knowing myself as a quicksand investment.
Picture me spiralling after the fullness
of zero, starved for the very same info
that's already jammed in my reservoir's overflow.

I contain multitudes, and it turns out I'm witless,
faced with as many dimensions as folded
layers of paper. Pretty soon, there's a limit.
Pretty soon, the striations get smoother,

slip off their framework, rescind their structure.
Selfhood brings all the confusions together:
a gutful of microbes and an over-clocked processor
swapping survival for nuance, or vice versa.

Reality

In another dream the night
before the workday,
I'm dappled with the rhetoric
of reality

like jots of boiled water
on my fingers
when I brew a cup of tea.
I must be better

at reality than a talking head
on the internet
—I water a plant, and mention it
to myself—

and though reality happens
unconsciously,
I'm also more real than the dreams
that haunt me

with a hint of deeper feeling.
So, I repeat:
I only think and speak
about reality.

A Plant is Not a Nation

Unlike a nation, a plant
can stick with its embarrassments enough
to grow more slowly
than the benchmark of accelerating annually.

Maybe it even refuses
to go on entirely. A plant will know its dirt
lands first on the dead and the un-
deserving. Unlike a nation

suspended in what it's saying, a plant
grows into the matter of history.
Look: you can cut open its leaves
and track the accident of its lifetime,

and a plant isn't bothered, doesn't mind.
A nation gives you nothing to cut into.
At best it's a shuffle of archives; at worst
a blade with no handle. Unlike a plant,

a nation is strong and free, and stands up
and sits others down from the perch
of a made-up hierarchy. Thank God a plant is not
a nation, living here on the bookshelf next to me.

My Houseplants'

leaves look like banana peels,
their thin skins like shadows.

Down there, it's almost all
matter, and the rest is rather small.

There's no question that I also wither;
it's just that my self-depth perception's better

at parsing green shoots of brain-
stem munching its material

and making mind a martyr
when it falls away.

Reality

A table, set, then cleared away
Reality is whatever we say

Its signature a sensation of slipping
Or skating over the surface of 'is'

We'd drown to wash our true depths clean
But truth is too heavy for reality

A paper computer unfolding indefinitely
Turn your back, reality is happening

It vivifies that awful excitement
Of swiftly peeling back the skin

The truths inside us contradict
But truth is too heavy for reality

Wikiholing
a hundred open windows

If Whitman says my mind is multitudes,
these hundred open windows on my desktop
(and their headings' nonstop shrinking
with each link I click) are equivalent

to the thickened middle of my thinking.
I follow consciousness notches in
a direction and rarely trace its steps;

it's better for reflection if
there's not much to look back at.
Wittgenstein: a keyword's substance
cuts off at the use I put it to—

a fuse of intellectual freestyles,
conceptualist tie-dyes set to blow
my whitebread head up with context.

I am the mind dissolved, a solution
to butchering more in half-sleep than a surname.
I daydream information like experience
without the responsibility,

and every signatory of every wiki
sings with me—for the truthless,
bottomless pit of the endlessly freed.

The Genuine Devil

The Devil celebrates
when others suffer

Though it isn't the suffering
he likes

He brims with excuses, his judgement's
on fire

But his heart's on ice

The Devil only instigates
passivity

He handles conflict with
outstanding care

He has no trouble winning
advocates

The games he plays are fair

The Devil doesn't flatter
to deceive

When he tells you he loves you, that's just
what he means

It isn't his business if it's un-
believable

He sings whatever praise
is most banal

The Devil doesn't want you
to be evil

He wants you to know how

Baffling Aphorisms

When I'm dreaming, I don't want anything
except to keep dreaming.

Sleep all night, sleep all day.

A dream: an experience without the responsibility.

Head on fire, heart on ice.

Thinking is thickening the middle.

Four Dreams About Justice

First I dreamt I was frenziedly searching
for the tiny spiral notebook I keep with me

at all times, except when I'm sleeping.
When I woke up I'd forgotten how to write,

so I only spoke aloud the second dreaming:
that tiny student here in our apartment

without entering, her phone a shard of cardstock
with an app that pinged a pack of Millennials

to crash: they threw an apartment party,
chopped up our refrigerator's veggies,

admired our balcony, clogged our bedroom
doorframe singing Disney karaoke,

and left—finally. But once we were alone,
the curl of time got stuck behind the stove clock

like a gum wad, and its spiral lost our heads.
I thought we'd never guess the hour again.

In the third dream, I'm in a car
with three men, poets—four softspoken men

with hard emotions, knowing we're poets the way
a dreamself knows a friend but not the person.

Opposite me in back, one's drunk
and hopeless. Riding shotgun's a backwards

stone face tablet flat, a man
my asking dies on. The last is panicked,

primed to drive to the moon—which is apt,
since none of us lets in a drink of the black

of night's Toronto. We're shut up as a womb,
and spaced out like in an airport waiting room.

We cruise through downtown blocks like basements
of the bungalows we all grew up in

before we learned to woo our brokenness
in cooler language, came into our own

as doughboys fudging half-baked histories
with the douchebag ease of the less guilty.

My friends' white faces are turning red;
white flags are waving. In my head, I muse,

"I read folks like I read words lately."
If we could have addressed each other, I might have said it.

But the fact is, I came here for another dreaming—
to talk, or type about it, and thus stretch it out,

since I've never really seen it or experienced it.
This fourth dream's dangling from my mouth.

It's a story I've boiled not down to, but free of its truth
in a kitchen as violently white as a tooth,

with no soft tissue to bite into.
In it, I manage a radical TAZ

with a quiet, white hand: some 12 blocks seceded
to a transparent image, to a good young man.

The cops are unwelcome. The rent has been cancelled.
We're doggedly woke, ethical, and equitable.

National leaders get frisked at our borders
by volunteer warriors, and visitors acknowledge

Indigenous land. State power uprooted,
grassroots communities heal their own conflicts,

the workers control the means of production,
and so on.

It's too bad that wasn't a real dream, but just
an idea I had, consciously—irony and all.

Forgive me: I can't help but ironize Justice
when Justice lies, white as a root or a bone,

and I find its fruit hanging so low. Although
it's also too bad I take Justice so seriously;

everyone knows I'd be better off dreaming.
I've never dreamt irony, really, just feeling,

and Justice has always been more of an idea
anyway, never enough to wake me.

Tubers

Funny how the blue one, Ophelia, survived,
her mad fate ossifying in the birdcage,
while the white-breasted, bald-headed
favourite died before his time, fleeing
his mantelpiece perch for our hardwood,
his instincts perverted, and getting KO'd
by the dog—

        a stupid thing
done stupidly. But they remind me
—I mean the corpse's marble eyes
—of Nana's blindness, her marbled mind,
her feathery whorl of hair recounting
the man I was in love with—what's his name?
—*well, he died*, and Mom, not at all surprised
by this, but surprised
when Ophelia grows her blushless cheek
a tumour fat and fuzzy as the disco.

At the street where buildings rub shoulders,
stargazing, and people dot the grid like fingerlings,
here is sound's austere symmetry broken
at one end. My father trades good sleep
to lose his memory; he's forgotten
the nature of exchange, and his deficit shunts downwards
like a taproot. Me? I'm bubbling,
potted under lid. My own roottips hit water
like a whisk.

Crass Aphorisms

Blessed are those who need not prove they're human,
for they can do something else entirely.

Give nonsense explanations, then ask for questions.

What's good news to bad people?

A life isn't much.

Some things I've learned to believe by disbelieving them
again and again.

Splits

I leave it to the ferns to decide
if the first duty of a life is to die

or to make die, since they split their stems.
Although we toke from the same pot,

we don't take the same breaths.
My family taught me that. A photo:

our simian faces bundled abominable—
three pea pods in the same pea plant.

It reminds me death is a sickness shed,
forever the outer element.

Its game is zero-sum. Thank God
(for now) we've won.

Object
to a houseplant

It's appropriate and possible
to freeze a gesture, just never mine.

The light, being itself material,
calls for material, and gives sight

and indication the form
of a line. But you don't rely

on it, just get caught
in a pirouette

as steadfast as a glacier
to a landscape. I keep saying

I learn from you or an apparition
of you *objectively*, as if

you took the many names
of a very small divinity,

so tiny
I could tear it apart in my hands.

Objects
to a houseplant

Gravity calls for its own landing
like gravestones call for the sky.

We're thrown along,
our bodies ragdolled,

all positions
declining to x.

Why would the sky rise, if not
for the weight of our skyless minds,

who only agree
to be helpless?

We are in propulsion, becoming
a more vastly disorganized mass.

Praise the God-slandering atoms;
all my votes go to the bootstrap.

I am building you a body
you'll outgrow again.

Praise God

"What I work to stay clear of & almost do is irony"
—Phil Hall, *Guthrie Clothing*

My God is not the Devil,
and that's enough for me.

I praise God without irony
and sing my praises honestly.

I praise the flavour of flavoured things
and do not believe in consistency—

What else would I have learned from Kanye?
I praise that I may write this wrongly,

That I may make a distinction at all.
I praise that I'm banal, but evil? Hardly.

I praise the right to live life falsely.
I believe that sunscreen will protect me,

That there's still a world in the cave.
I praise that we'll all die eventually,

Praise God for resembling His enemy
and letting me disbelieve.

```
                    Oo _ A
                 _ - \oUA _ o
               (~ J l \°\{ i>_>()
               c*x -a*@C _> ---o
               {_} c V \\(  j ;
                (_ / "( '/ L \ ~,
                (,,J  ( )   (_ J


  ,,;_ k<
  `  vK<-.
    / / ~
   // lk-,
 *>>=< wK
 j/*l*yA\E< ,
 .>\k/"/ vk,:=<
 j/ >- K-v `
   ~ \.lkW
       * X
       ( k




                    b         {}
                 U    w {} ,  vA
                    ~~  k/  J/c=
                    w` \ }  >C
                       A{ }`  X
              mm^ _ { / ~
               uU  e
                   kma
```

```
                A
        _    A  A
        -.  V  V /      __
     .-Jh-->rl  k ~`  ~ `
      ._   j x>73 F*=_- >
         >` ,/| / ) \ W- >
       V v  |f `   `  J,
            v




                              ( (D
                        u.  V
                          \
                            A
                            U




            )  ||
       _       /  //
       \ \       // //
     ___\ \  Jxa///
 ___  ~===} @SWL__  ~~~ `
~` ` ||   V} { \ \ ~-- /
      `  / {  | \ \
        /{ | L \ \
        / { ||    \\
        J  ||      \
           |
```

Notes

The epigraph from Aristotle's *Metaphysics* is from the translation by W. D. Ross.

The epigraph from Plato's *Symposium* is from the translation by Alexander Nehamas and Paul Woodruff.

"I" adapts Gilles Deleuze and Félix Guattari's *A Thousand Plateaus*: "Many people have a tree growing in their heads, but the brain itself is much more a grass than a tree." *Beyond Good and Evil* was written by Friedrich Nietzsche.

In "Backwards Aphorisms," the italicized lines are from songs by Tame Impala.

The short film described in "Life-Death" is *La Impresión de una guerra* (Impression of a war) by Camilo Restrepo.

"Laughable Aphorisms" adapts Gertrude Stein: "A rose is a rose is a rose."

"Touch-Me-Not" refers to the touch-me-not or sensitive plant (*Mimosa pudica*), a tropical weed whose leaves quickly fold closed when touched or shaken.

"The Devil's Intelligence" borrows from Tristan Tzara: "Thought is made in the mouth."

"It's Mine" mentions Joseph Ducreux's 1783 portrait of himself yawning. It also alludes to his *Portrait de l'artiste sous les traits d'un moqueur* (1793), which is a popular meme image.

"Horns" adapts Martin Niemöller's confession of his inaction during Hitler's rise to power, which has been published in many variations.

For example:

> First they came for the socialists, and I did not speak out—
> Because I was not a socialist.
>
> Then they came for the trade unionists, and I did not speak out—
> Because I was not a trade unionist.
>
> Then they came for the Jews, and I did not speak out—
> Because I was not a Jew.
>
> Then they came for me—and there was no one left to speak for me.

In "Sad Aphorisms," the italicized lines are from Amanda Ackerman's *The Book of Feral Flora*.

"Wikihole" alludes to Walt Whitman's "Song of Myself":

> Do I contradict myself?
> Very well then I contradict myself,
> (I am large, I contain multitudes.)

"A Plant is Not a Nation" is indebted to Rabindranath Tagore: "A mind all logic is like a knife all blade, it makes the hand bleed that uses it."

"Wikiholing" alludes to Ludwig Wittgenstein's *Philosophical Investigations*: "the meaning of a word is its use in the language."

In "Four Dreams About Justice," TAZ stands for Temporary Autonomous Zone, as theorized by Hakim Bey.

"Praise God" alludes to the Allegory of the Cave from Plato's *Republic*, as well as Hannah Arendt's *Eichmann in Jerusalem: A Report on the Banality of Evil*.

Acknowledgements

Looking back over 7+ years of work on this book, I'm astounded by how many friends and acquaintances have contributed their eyes, ears, and voices to its development. Many thanks to those who read and responded to early drafts of these poems, including Gary Barwin, Jason Boissonneault, Mike Chaulk, Miles Forrester, Kevin Andrew Heslop, Jeremy Luke Hill, William Hunt, Jo Ianni, Hostyn James, Kirby, Michael Kleiza, Lauren Lavery, Annick MacAskill, Cassidy McFadzean, Khashayar Mohammadi, Sierra Paquette-Struger, Terese Mason Pierre, Larissa Tiggelers, Ksenija Spasić, Bieke Stengos, and anyone else I've forgotten. Many thanks also to anyone who listened to performances of these poems and offered feedback—your presence keeps me writing.

Special thanks to my first and best reader, Amanda Boulos, for her love, encouragement, and criticism. Special thanks to Jim Johnstone, whose dedication to the craft and cultivation of poetry is unparalleled in this country. And special thanks to Aimée Parent Dunn for her tireless efforts making books.

Previous versions of these poems have appeared in *Rampike*, *The Malahat Review*, *EVENT*, *The /tɛmz/ Review*, the Penteract Press nanopamphlet *Two Houseplants, from above* (2019), and the knife | fork | book chapbook *The Devil* (2020). My thanks to the editors and publishers.

Finally, thanks to the Ontario Arts Council (OAC) for their financial support of this project via the Recommender Grants for Writers program, and to the recommenders who selected my work.

Photo by Brent Rose

John Nyman is a poet, critic, and book artist of mixed European and Ashkenazi Jewish ancestry. His previous works include a Gerald Lampert Award-shortlisted poetry collection (*Players*), an erasure of words and images from the Choose Your Own Adventure series of children's books (*Your Very Own*), and a classic text of Lacanian psycho-analysis reprinted in a nearly illegible typeface (*The Four Fundamental Concepts of Psycho analysis: A Selection*). John hails from Tkaronto/Toronto, where he currently works as a postsecondary communication instructor and helps administer the plumb art gallery and project space on St. Clair West. Find him online at johnnyman.ca